I·N·S·I·D·E

MEXICO

Ian James

Franklin Watts

London · New York · Sydney · Toronto

CONTENTS

© 1989 Franklin Watts
12a Golden Square
London W1

Published in the USA by
Franklin Watts Inc.
387 Park Avenue South
New York, N.Y. 10016

Franklin Watts Australia
14 Mars Road
Lane Cove
NSW 2066

Design: Edward Kinsey
Illustrations: Hayward Art Group

UK ISBN: 0 86313 835 7
US ISBN: 0-531-10640-3
Library of Congress Catalog
Card Number: 88-50362

Phototypeset by Lineage Ltd, Watford
Printed in Belgium

Additional Photographs:
Chris Fairclough 30; Hutchison 15, 24B,
25, 27, 29; Keith Lye 8A, 8B; Tony Morrison
4, 5A, 6, 7, 9, 10, 11A, 16, 17, 18A, 18B,
19, 21, 22, 23, 24A, 26, 28; ZEFA 5B, 11B, 20

Front cover: Tony Morrison
Back cover: ZEFA
Frontispiece: ZEFA

The land

Mexico is a republic in North America. It is officially called the United Mexican States, and consists of 31 States and one Federal District (for the capital, Mexico City). It faces the Gulf of Mexico and the Caribbean Sea in the east and the Pacific Ocean in the west.

Most Mexicans live on the central plateau running from the United States border to south of Mexico City. It is bordered by two mountain ranges: the Sierra Madre Occidental in the west and the Sierra Madre Oriental in the east. The southern plateau contains many volcanoes, including Citlaltépetl, Mexico's highest peak. Northern Mexico contains two other areas: the Pacific northwest, which includes Lower, or Baja, California, and the coastal plains along the Gulf of Mexico.

Below: **Mexico's Pacific coast contains many attractive sandy beaches.**

Above: **The volcano Citlaltépetl, which is also called Orizaba, is Mexico's highest peak.**

Left: **Rugged mountain ranges border the central plateau of Mexico**

The Yucatán Peninsula, in the southeast, consists of a low, limestone plateau. Rainwater has worn out deep pits in the rock which lead to caves and underground rivers. Southwestern Mexico is mountainous. The main range is the Sierra Madre del Sur.

The climate varies greatly. The coastlands are warm, but the land between 900 and 1,800 m (2,953-5,906 ft) has a mild climate. Higher areas are cool and many mountains are always snow-capped. The north is dry with areas of desert and semi-desert. Most of the central plateau land mountains have enough rain for farming. The tropical south is the rainiest region. Hurricanes occasionally hit the east coast of Mexico causing much damage.

Above: **Forests grow on wet mountain slopes and in the rainy tropical south.**

The people and their history

American Indians were probably living in Mexico by 10,000BC. By 1500BC, they could irrigate the land and grow crops. About 2,500 years ago, great civilizations began to develop and later on, huge, flat-topped pyramids were built. The best known Indian civilizations were those of the Mayans in the south and the Aztecs. The Aztec capital was on the site of Mexico City.

Spanish soldiers conquered the Aztecs between 1519 and 1521 and Spain ruled Mexico until 1821. Because of intermarriage, most Mexicans today are *mestizos* (people of mixed Spanish and Indian origin). Spanish is Mexico's official language, though many Indian languages are also spoken. Most Mexicans are Roman Catholics.

Below: **This steep-sided pyramid is one of the beautiful buildings in the ancient Mayan city of Palenque in southern Mexico.**

7

Left: **This mural painted by the Mexican artist Diego Rivera shows ancient Indian artists at work.**

Below: *The Shooting of Emperor Maximilian*, **drawn by Diego Rivera. Maximilian served as emperor between 1864 and 1867.**

Mexico became a republic in 1824. In 1836, it lost Texas, which became part of the United States in 1845. Mexico and the United States were at war from 1846 to 1848 and by its end large areas of Mexico were taken by the United States.

War ruined Mexico's economy and in the early 1860s, Mexico delayed payments of money owed to Britain, France and Spain. France invaded Mexico and made Maximilian emperor of Mexico. But when the French troops left in 1867, Maximilian was shot.

In the late 19th century, revolutionary groups sprang up among the poor. The Mexican Revolution began in 1910 and, in 1929, several groups formed the Revolutionary Party, which has ruled Mexico ever since.

Below: **The National Palace in Mexico City is on the site of the palace of the Aztec emperor Montezuma. It contains the offices of Mexico's President.**

Towns and cities

The most thickly populated part of Mexico is the southern part of the fertile central plateau. In this area are two of the country's largest cities: the capital, Mexico City, which is the world's largest and fastest growing city, and Guadalajara, to the northwest of Mexico City. The third largest city, Monterrey, is in the northeast, not far from the border with the United States.

Most settlements in Mexico were originally founded by the Indians. But they were rebuilt and enlarged by the Spaniards. A typical feature of most towns, cities and even villages is a central *plaza* (square), where the main church and government buildings stand. The plazas, where people come to sit and talk with their friends, have a very Spanish atmosphere.

Below: **Many villages lack services, including paved roads.**

Above: **The silver mining town of Taxco, south of Mexico City, has a strong Spanish atmosphere.**

Left: **Guadalajara, Mexico's second largest city, has much modern architecture, as well as many fine old buildings.**

Mexico's population has risen from 15 million in 1910 to more than 80 million in the mid-1980s. In the early 1980s, the country's population was increasing by 2.6 percent per year, far higher than the world average of 1.8 percent. At this rate, Mexico's population would double in less than 30 years.

In 1985, 69 percent of Mexicans lived in towns and cities, as compared with 55 percent in 1965. Many country people have moved to the cities in search of jobs and better schools and hospitals. But the cities have not been able to house all the newcomers and huge slums have grown up, especially around Mexico City. The fast growth of the cities has caused other problems, including traffic jams and severe pollution.

Below: **Acapulco, on the southwestern coast of Mexico, is the country's best known resort.**

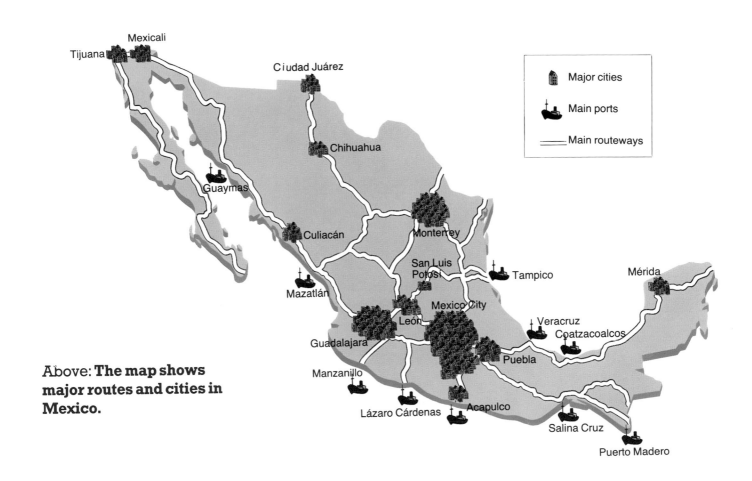

Above: **The map shows major routes and cities in Mexico.**

Tijuana
Mexicali
Ciudad Juárez
Chihuahua
Guaymas
Culiacán
Monterrey
Mazatlán
San Luis Potosí
Tampico
Mérida
Mexico City
León
Veracruz
Coatzacoalcos
Guadalajara
Puebla
Manzanillo
Lázaro Cárdenas
Acapulco
Salina Cruz
Puerto Madero

Major cities
Main ports
Main routeways

Right: **Mexico City was hit by a severe earthquake in 1985. Many buildings were damaged.**

More than 18 million people live in Mexico City and its suburbs. It is a major tourist city, with many industries and educational institutions. It stands at 2,310 m (7,579 ft) above sea level on the site of Tenochtitlán, the Aztec capital, which was surrounded by a lake. As Mexico City grew, the Spaniards drained the lake and built on its bed. In 1985 an earthquake violently shook the rocks of the old lake bed. Buildings collapsed and over 7,000 people died.

The city has many beautiful, historic places. The central Zócalo (Constitution Plaza) contains the National Palace and the National Cathedral. The fascinating Square of the Three Cultures contains a mixture of Aztec, Spanish and modern buildings. The Museum of Anthropology has many ancient treasures.

The maps show some of Mexico City's landmarks.

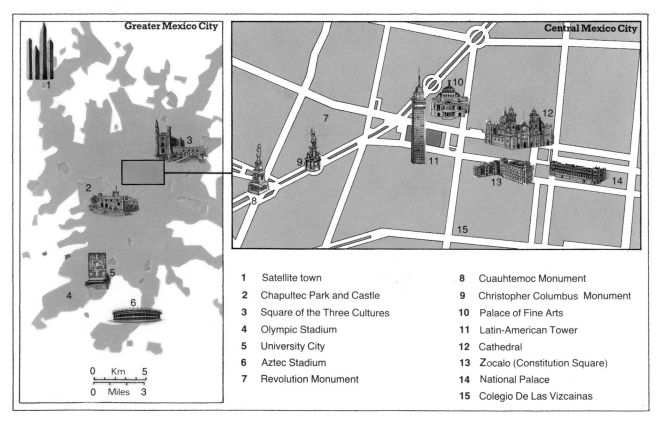

1	Satellite town	**8**	Cuauhtemoc Monument
2	Chapultec Park and Castle	**9**	Christopher Columbus Monument
3	Square of the Three Cultures	**10**	Palace of Fine Arts
4	Olympic Stadium	**11**	Latin-American Tower
5	University City	**12**	Cathedral
6	Aztec Stadium	**13**	Zocalo (Constitution Square)
7	Revolution Monument	**14**	National Palace
		15	Colegio De Las Vizcainas

Family life

Above: **Mothers often carry babies on their backs when they go shopping.**

Homes in Mexico vary greatly from elegant houses and modern city apartments to self-built shacks in the shanty towns and simple village houses with walls of wood or clay. On average, Mexicans are much less prosperous than people in the United States. For example, only a quarter of Mexican households own a car.

The average number of people in a household is six and households often include people of three generations. Family ties are close and most people live with their parents until they marry. Girls generally have less freedom than boys, but more and more girls in the cities are being educated for jobs in factories, offices or in the professions.

15

Above: **New apartment buildings have been built in Mexico City to house some of the fast increasing population.**

Left: **Middle class families in the cities have comfortable homes.**

Food

For many Mexicans, breakfast consists of coffee with bread or pastries. Lunch is the main meal in rural areas, but in cities, the main family meal of the day is in the evening.

Some well-known Mexican dishes are made from *tortillas*, which are flat pancakes made from maize (or corn) meal. For example, *tacos* are folded tortillas containing various fillings, *enchiladas* are rolled up tortillas with fillings, and *tostadas* are tortillas that are deep-fried until they are crisp and served with beans, meat and salad. Other dishes include *chili con carne* (spicy meat and beans), *frijoles* (boiled beans which are mashed and fried), *guacamole* (avocado dip), and *mole poblano* (chicken or turkey with a brown sauce, or *mole*, containing unsweetened chocolate).

Below: **Most towns have large indoor markets where all kinds of fresh food are on sale.**

Above: **A cook is putting fillings into tortillas.**

Left: **Meals in restaurants are special family occasions. Children often drink fruit juices while adults drink wine or beer.**

Sports and pastimes

As in other Latin American countries, the leading spectator sport is soccer and the soccer World Cup finals of 1970 and 1986 were held in Mexico. Some popular sports, such as bullfighting, were introduced by Spaniards. The first bullfight in Mexico took place in the 1520s and Mexico City has the world's largest bullfighting ring. Another sport, which comes from Spain, is *jai alai*, a fast game in which players hit a ball against a wall with a racket. Other sports, like baseball, originated in the United States.

Swimming, tennis and volleyball are other popular sports, while golf, polo and yachting are enjoyed by richer people. Jogging and walking are the chief ways in which city people try to keep fit.

Below: **A bullfight in the huge Plaza de Toros Monumental in Mexico City.**

Mexico has many festivals. Some are national holidays, while others are local fiestas, when people celebrate their patron saint. Popular activities on fiesta days include rodeos or charreadas, firework displays, music and dancing. One unusual festival is the Day of the Dead, when Indians believe that the souls of their dead relatives return to visit them.

Major national holidays include Independence Day on September 16, an occasion for parades, and Christmas. One Christmas custom is the *piñata* game. *Piñatas* are containers filled with toys and things to eat. They are hung from the ceiling and blindfolded children try to break them with a stick to release their contents.

Above: **Mexican dancers wear Aztec-style clothes at fiestas and pageants.**

The arts

The ancient Indians were great architects. They built superb flat-topped pyramids and stone temples, which were decorated with carvings of gods and large murals (wall paintings). Some of the finest buildings were constructed by the Mayan Indians in the Yucatán peninsula between about AD 250 and 900, and by the Toltec Indians who conquered the Mayans in about 950 and who flourished until about 1200. The Aztecs, who dominated central Mexico from the 13th century until 1521, created some fine sculptures. They also wrote poetry and composed music.

Spain provided an important influence in Mexican culture. Spanish architects are known for their graceful churches. Settlers in colonial times also contributed to Spanish literature.

Below: **The Atlantes are huge carved columns of rock which represent warriors. They were sculpted by Toltec Indians at Tula, in central Mexico, in about AD 900.**

Several modern Mexican painters are known for their murals. The founder of the modern school of mural painting, Diego Rivera, painted scenes of ancient Indian life and works about Mexican history and the Revolution. Other mural painters were José Clemente Orozco and David Alfaro Siqueiros.

Mexican writers have contributed much to world literature. The best known modern novelist is Carlos Fuentes. His works have been translated into many languages. Octavio Paz, the poet and essayist, has shed much light on the character of Mexican people. Mexico also has a long tradition of music. The modern composer Carlos Chávez often used themes from folk music in his work.

Above: **Diego Rivera, Mexico's best known painter, often used political images in his murals.**

Farming

Farmland covers 12 percent of the land and meadows and pastures another 39 percent. The chief crop is maize (or corn) which is grown on 43 percent of the cultivated land. Beans, coffee, cotton, sugar cane and wheat are other leading crops. Beef cattle are grazed in the drier north, while dairy cattle are more important in the southern part of the central plateau. Large numbers of goats, horses, pigs, poultry and sheep are also reared. Farming employs 37 percent of Mexico's workforce.

Forests cover 24 percent of the land. Pine trees are used to make wood pulp and paper, and sapodilla trees in the south provide chicle, which is used to make chewing gum. Fishing is another important industry and shrimp and prawns are exported.

Below: **Farmers collect stubble from maize (corn) fields and use it to feed their cattle.**

Left: **Children often help their parents by taking care of the farm animals.**

Below: **Butterfly nets are often used to catch fish in inland waters.**

Industry

Before the 1910 Revolution, Mexico was a poor farming country. But since then, the number of industries has steadily increased, especially since the 1940s. Industry now employs 29 percent of the workforce and the United Nations now describes Mexico as an upper middle-income, developing country.

The country has deposits of many metals, including copper, gold, lead and silver. It also produces coal and the nuclear fuel, uranium. Oil is extracted along the east coast and from offshore wells in the Gulf of Mexico. In 1987, Mexico was the world's fourth largest oil producer. Mexico has many hydroelectric power stations. They produce about one third of the country's electricity supply.

Above: **Many oil wells lie offshore in the Gulf of Mexico. Unwanted natural gas is burned off.**

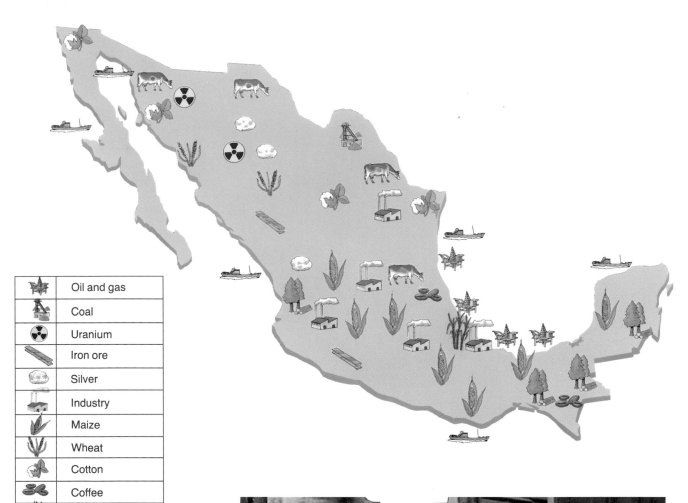

	Oil and gas
	Coal
	Uranium
	Iron ore
	Silver
	Industry
	Maize
	Wheat
	Cotton
	Coffee
	Sugar cane
	Cattle
	Fishing port
	Forestry

Above: **The map shows some of the economic activities in Mexico.**

Right: **Young people are trained in rural crafts.**

Mexico City, Monterrey and Guadalajara are the leading industrial cities. Products include processed food and beverages, chemicals, metals and metal products, oil products, textiles and clothing, and transport equipment. Many craft workers make beautiful glassware, pottery, silverware and textiles, mainly for sale to tourists, who numbered 4,625,000 in 1986.

Oil accounts for nearly two-thirds of the exports. The United States is Mexico's leading trading partner and imports many low-cost manufactured goods. These products are cheap, because wages in Mexican factories are lower than in the United States.

Above: **Car making and assembly are an important industry in Mexico.**

27

Looking to the future

As oil exports rose in the 1960s, Mexico prospered. The government borrowed money to modernize the oil industry and to create new industries. But since the mid-1970s, the world demand for oil has fallen, as has the price paid for a barrel of oil.

Mexico's income declined and the government found it hard to pay the interest on the money it had borrowed. Inflation rose, averaging 64 percent a year between 1980 and 1986, and the real wages of most people fell. Big cuts in government spending, led to increased unemployment. Many Mexicans went to the United States in search of jobs. This caused problems between the two countries, because many Mexicans entered the United States illegally.

Below: **People demonstrate against the government in Mexico City.**

In tackling its many economic problems, Mexico has many advantages. It has plenty of natural resources and, unlike many Latin American countries, Mexico has a stable government — the Revolutionary Party has been in office since 1929. Mexico also has great human resources.

The population of Mexico is young — 43 percent are under 15 years of age and 70 percent are under 30. Primary and secondary education is free and compulsory. By the 1980s, Mexico's universities contained more than a million students. These young, energetic people are determined to help eliminate poverty and to transform Mexico into a developed country.

Above: **Young people believe that education is the key to most of Mexico's problems.**

Facts about Mexico

Area:
1,972,547 sq km
(761,605 sq miles)

Population:
81,861,000 (1987)

Capital:
Mexico City

Largest cities:
Mexico City (pop with
    suburbs, 18,748,000)
Guadalajara (2,245,000)
Monterrey (1,916,000)
Puebla (836,000)
León (656,000)
Ciudad Juárez (567,000)
Culiacán (560,000)

Official language:
Spanish

Religion:
Christianity (Roman
Catholics make up
93 percent of the
population)

Main exports:
Oil and oil products,
metals, vehicles,
various farm products.

Unit of currency:
Peso

Mexico compared with other countries

Mexico 42 per sq km

Britain 232 per sq km

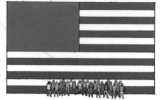

USA 26 per sq km

Australia 2 per sq km

Above: **How many people?**
Mexico is more densely
populated than the United
States.

Below: **How large?**
Mexico is smaller than the
United States but larger
than most European
countries.

USA   **Australia**

Mexico   **UK**

Below: **Some Mexican**
money and stamps.

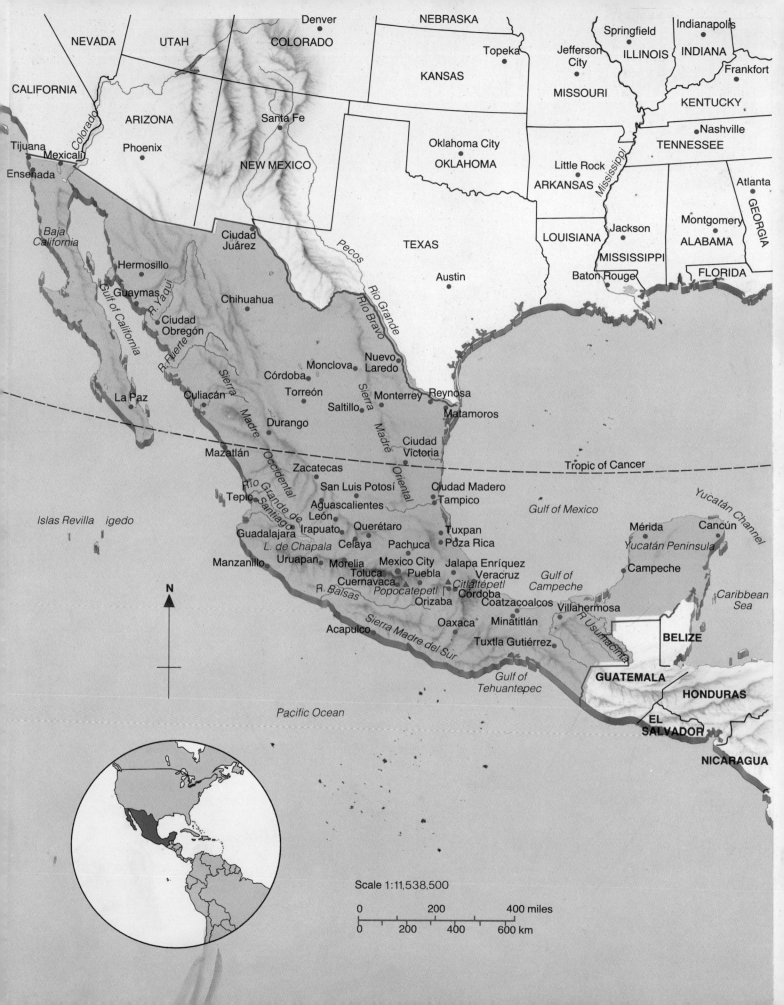

Index

PRINTED IN BELGIUM BY

proost
INTERNATIONAL BOOK PRODUCTION